Why do fawns have spots?

Jinny Johnson

Miles
Kelly

First published in 2011 by Miles Kelly Publishing Ltd
Harding's Barn, Bardfield End Green, Thaxted,
Essex, CM6 3PX, UK

2 4 6 8 10 9 7 5 3

Publishing Director Belinda Gallagher
Creative Director Jo Cowan
Editorial Director Rosie McGuire
Editor Claire Philip
Volume Designer Sally Lace
Cover Designer Kayleigh Allen
Image Manager Liberty Newton
Indexer Gill Lee
Production Manager Elizabeth Collins
Reprographics Anthony Cambray, Stephan Davis
Assets Lorraine King, Cathy Miles

ISBN 978-1-84810-455-6

Printed in China

British Library Cataloguing-in-Publication Data

A catalogue record for this book is
available from the British Library

ACKNOWLEDGEMENTS
The publishers would like to thank the following
artist who has contributed to this book:

Mike Foster (character cartoons)

All other artwork from the Miles Kelly Artwork Bank

The publishers would like to thank the following
sources for the use of their photographs:

Dreamstime.com 19 Steve Byland; 25 Drpramodb
iStockphoto.com 26 hilton123
Shutterstock.com 4–5 Kitch Bain; 7 tratong;
8 THP/Tim Hester Photography;
9 Benjamin Albiach Galan; 11 Kane513;
13 Meewezen Photography; 22 Hedrus

All other photographs are from:
digitalvision, PhotoDisc

Every effort has been made to acknowledge the
source and copyright holder of each picture.
Miles Kelly Publishing apologises for any unintentional
errors or omissions.

Made with paper from a sustainable forest

www.mileskelly.net
info@mileskelly.net

www.factsforprojects.com

Self-publish your
children's book

buddingpress.co.uk

contents

Which animal is the best mum?   4

Which frog is the best dad?   5

What do baby frogs look like?   5

Why do fawns have spots?   6

How do monkeys clean their babies?   7

What do baby sharks eat?   7

Why do kangaroos have pouches?   8

Are turtles born in the sea?   9

Which animal has the longest pregnancy?   9

Why do baby animals play?   10

Which bird makes the biggest nest?   11

Are baby snakes dangerous?   11

where do baby rabbits live? 12

when can foals walk? 13

Do baby animals laugh? 13

How do polar bear cubs keep warm? 14

when do caterpillars become butterflies? 15

why do scorpions carry their young? 15

When can squirrels leave their nests? 16

why do spiders leave home? 17

Do sharks lay eggs? 17

Do sloths give birth upside down? 18

How do penguin chicks keep warm? 19

How do baby birds get food? 19

Do baby elephants leave their herd? 20

How does a chick get out of its egg? 21

Do badgers keep their nests clean? 21

why do lion cubs play fight? 22

Do snakes lay eggs? 23

why are some eggs pear-shaped? 23

When do fox cubs leave their dens? 24

Why do cuckoos lay eggs quickly? 25

which bird has the safest nest? 25

When can cheetah cubs live alone? 26

Why are harp seal pups white? 27

what do baby pandas eat? 27

can rhino mums be fierce? 28

Are baby hedgehogs born prickly? 29

Are alligators good parents? 29

Quiz time 30

Index 32

Which animal is the best mum?

Many animals take great care of their young, but the orang-utan is one of the most caring. They feed their babies for at least three years and cuddle up close every night. A young orang-utan stays with its mum until it is about seven or eight years old.

Baby orang-utan

Big eater!
A baby blue whale drinks nearly 400 litres of its mother's milk every day. That's about five bathfuls!

which frog is the best dad?

The green poison-dart frog is! The male guards his eggs while they develop. Then, after the eggs have hatched into tadpoles, he takes them to a safe pool of water to grow.

Tadpoles

Green poison-dart frog

Find

What did you look like as a baby? Find some photos of you when you were a few months old.

what do baby frogs look like?

Baby frogs, called tadpoles, look very different from their parents. They are little swimming creatures with a tail and no legs. They have gills for breathing in water. As they get bigger, tadpoles grow legs and lose their tail.

Why do fawns have spots?

The spotty coat of a fawn (baby deer) makes it hard to see in its forest home. This is because the sun shines through leaves and twigs, making light spots on the forest floor — just like the spots on the fawn's coat.

Imagine
Pretend you are a mother bird and make a soft nest using blankets and pillows.

Fawn

How do monkeys clean their babies?

Monkeys groom their young with their fingers and pick out bits of dead skin, insects and dirt. Many animals also lick their babies to keep them clean.

Macaque monkey family

Trunk call

Elephants use their trunks for many things, such as grabbing food from trees. Baby elephants have to learn to control their trunks.

What do baby sharks eat?

Some eat other baby sharks! The eggs of the sand tiger shark hatch inside the mother's body. The first young to hatch then feed on the other eggs. When the sharks are born they are about one metre long.

Why do kangaroos have pouches?

Kangaroos have pouches to keep their babies safe. A baby kangaroo is called a joey and it is very weak and tiny when it is born. It lives in its mum's pouch where it feeds and grows until it is strong enough to look after itself.

Joey

Think

Puppy, kitten, chick... how many other names for baby animals can you think of?

Baby loggerhead turtle

Are turtles born in the sea?

Turtles live in the sea but lay their eggs on land. The mother turtle crawls up onto the beach and digs a pit in which to lay her eggs. When the eggs hatch, the babies make their way down to the sea.

Which animal has the longest pregnancy?

Pregnancy is the word used for the time it takes for a baby to grow inside its mother. The female elephant has the longest pregnancy of any animal – up to 21 months – that's nearly two years!

Watch out!

Family life is dangerous for the praying mantis, a type of insect. The mum is bigger than the dad – and she often eats him!

Why do baby animals play?

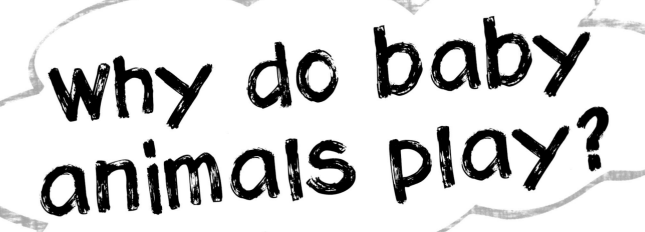

Lots of baby animals, such as otters pups, love to play. It helps them grow stronger and learn skills they will need as adults. Play fighting and chasing helps young animals learn how to hunt and catch prey.

Otter pups

which bird makes the biggest nest?

The bald eagle makes the biggest nest of any bird. The largest ever seen was about 6 metres deep – big enough for a giraffe to hide in! The eagles use the same nest every year and add more sticks to it each time.

Bald eagle in its nest

Biggest egg

The ostrich lays the biggest egg of any bird. It weighs more than 1.5 kg – that's the same as 24 hen's eggs!

Are baby snakes dangerous?

Some are, yes. Not all types of snake use venom to kill their prey, but those that do, such as rattlesnakes, can give a deadly bite soon after they are born.

Ask
Find out how much you weighed at birth and measure out the same amount using weighing scales.

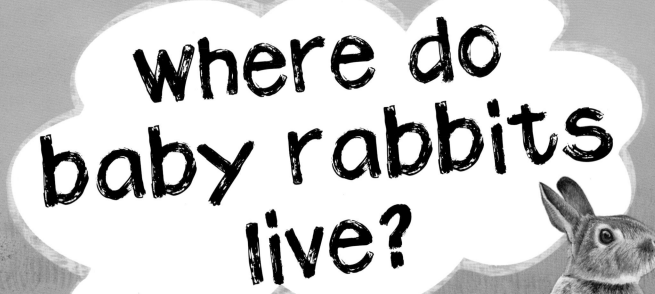

where do baby rabbits live?

Baby rabbits are called kits and they live in a cosy nest called a warren. The warren is underground and lined with hay, straw and fur to help keep the kits warm.

Warren

Kits

when can foals walk?

Just a few hours after they are born! Foals need to be able to walk soon after birth, as in the wild they may have to escape from animals that might hunt them. Foals also stay close to their mums for safety.

Foal

Greedy!

Caterpillars spend all their time eating and can grow to more than 30,000 times the size they were when they hatched!

Draw

What does your favourite baby animal look like? Once you have decided, draw a picture.

Do baby animals laugh?

Some do! Gorillas, chimps and orang-utans laugh when they're playing or tickling each other, just like we do. Scientists think that some other animals, such as dogs, may also laugh.

How do polar bear cubs keep warm?

Polar bear cubs

Polar bears live in the Arctic, where it is always very cold. The mother bear digs a den under the snow where her cubs are born. They live there until they are three months old. It is surprisingly warm and cosy in the den!

Play

Would you be a good mum or dad? Pretend your teddy bear is a baby and look after it carefully all day.

① Caterpillar hatches from its egg

② Pupa is formed

③ Butterfly breaks out of its pupa

when do caterpillars become butterflies?

When a caterpillar has grown as big as it can, it stops eating and makes a hard case around itself called a pupa. Inside the pupa the caterpillar's body changes into a butterfly. The butterfly then breaks out of the pupa and flies away.

④ Butterfly flies away

Big baby

Blue whales have the world's biggest babies. They are about 8 metres long at birth – that's roughly as long as two cars!

Why do scorpions carry their young?

Scorpions carry their babies on their backs until they are big and strong enough to take care of themselves. They climb onto their mum's back when they hatch and are carried around for the first two weeks.

When can squirrels leave their nests?

Baby squirrels are born tiny and helpless with very little fur. They stay in their tree trunk nest for seven to ten weeks, feeding and growing. By ten weeks they are nearly fully grown and can look after themselves.

Mother and baby squirrels

Why do spiders leave home?

Baby spiders are called spiderlings, and as they grow they need to move to new areas to find food. Each spider spins silken threads from the tip of its body. These catch the air like kites and carry the spider to a new home.

Think

Try to think of as many different animals that make nests and draw pictures of them.

Tall tales

Giraffes are the tallest of all animals. Even a newborn giraffe is around 1.8 metres tall – that's as big as a grown-up person!

Shark egg

Do sharks lay eggs?

Some sharks do. Each egg grows in a strong case, sometimes called a mermaid's purse. The case has long threads that attach to seaweed or rocks to help keep it safe.

Egg case

Shark pup

Do sloths give birth upside down?

Yes, they do! Sloths give birth to their babies hanging upside down from trees! The baby then stays close to its mother, clinging to her fur for the first nine months of its life.

Sloth mother and baby

Make

Use some play dough to make a bird's nest and then make some little eggs to place inside.

Queen bee

A queen honeybee lays all the eggs for her hive but she doesn't look after them, The worker bees take care of the babies for her!

How do penguin chicks keep warm?

Penguins usually live in cold places and keep warm by huddling together – the chicks stand on their parents feet. The penguins keep swapping places so each gets a turn at being in the middle – the warmest spot.

How do baby birds get food?

Most baby birds are fed by their parents. Adult birds work very hard to find tasty morsels to bring back to their chicks. The babies always seem to be hungry and wait with their beaks wide open.

Mother bird and chick

Do baby elephants leave their herd?

Only male elephants ever leave their close family groups, called herds. Young elephants stay with their mums for many years. The males will eventually leave and live alone or with other males, but females stay with their herd.

Elephant mother

Calf

Make

Find lots of pictures of baby animals. Stick them on a big sheet of paper to make a poster.

How does a chick get out of its egg?

A baby bird has a tiny spike, called an egg tooth, on its beak. When it is ready to hatch, the chick makes a little hole in the shell with the egg tooth and then struggles out.

Chick breaking out

Egg

Busy mum

Virginia opossums can have up to 13 babies at a time. The babies are tiny at birth and stay with their mum for about three months.

Do badgers keep their nests clean?

Yes they do. Badgers live in underground nests called setts, and use grass, leaves and straw for bedding. The badgers bring their bedding out of the sett to air it and then throw out old, dirty bedding.

Why do lion cubs play fight?

To practise the hunting skills they have learnt from their mothers. Female lions train their cubs to hunt by bringing small animals for the cubs to catch. Then the young lions go and watch their mothers hunting from a safe distance.

Lion cubs play fighting

① Baby snake breaking eggshell

② Fully hatched

Do snakes lay eggs?

Most snakes do lay eggs, although some give birth to live babies. A snake's eggshell is tough, bendy and almost watertight, unlike a hen's egg. Female snakes usually lay about five to 20 eggs at a time.

Big mouth

The mouth brooder fish keeps its eggs safe in its mouth while they develop and grow.

Why are some eggs pear-shaped?

A guillemot is a type of sea bird that nests on cliffs. Its eggs are pear-shaped with one end more pointed than the other. This shape means that the egg rolls round in a circle if knocked, and won't roll off the cliff.

Paint

Ask an adult to hard-boil some eggs for you. Then paint pictures on the shells.

When do fox cubs leave their dens?

Fox cubs are born blind and helpless so they stay in their dens for the first few weeks. If their home is disturbed, the mother fox may move her cubs to a new den. Most cubs make their first outing when they are four weeks old.

Fox cubs

why do cuckoos lay eggs quickly?

Because they lay their eggs in other birds' nests, instead of making their own. The other bird then looks after and feeds the cuckoo chick. A cuckoo lays an egg in just nine seconds – most birds take several minutes!

clever baby

A gorilla baby develops more quickly than a human baby. They can crawl at about two months and walk at nine months.

Think

When human babies want their parents they cry. What noise do you think a baby bird makes to get attention?

which bird has the safest nest?

The female hornbill makes her nest in a tree hole. The male then blocks up the hole with mud so that she and the eggs are safe from hunters. He leaves a hole for her beak so he can feed her while she's inside.

Male hornbill feeding female

when can cheetah cubs live alone?

Cheetah cubs can live alone when they are about 18 months old. Before they are ready to leave their mother they must learn to catch their own food. They learn how to hunt by watching their mother.

Cheetah cubs

Why are harp seal pups white?

Harp seals live in the snowy Arctic. The pups have white coats to keep them hidden from polar bears, which hunt them. Their fluffy coats also help to keep the seal pups warm.

Harp seal pup

What do baby pandas eat?

A baby panda drinks its mother's milk until it is about nine months old. Adult pandas feed on bamboo, and the baby starts to eat this when it is about six months old.

Discover
Some baby wasps feed on dung – animal poo! Find out what some other baby animals like to eat.

Marvellous mum
An octopus is a great mum. She guards her eggs for about a month while they grow, and she doesn't even leave them to find food.

can rhino mums be fierce?

Yes they can – a rhino mum can be fierce when she's looking after her young. If hyaenas or other animals try to attack her baby, she charges towards them with her sharp horn to scare them away.

Rhino mum and calf

Are baby hedgehogs born prickly?

Luckily for hedgehog mums, their babies' have very soft spines at first. They harden as the baby grows until they are extremely sharp and strong.

Find out

Ask your parents how old you were when you could first crawl, walk and talk.

Are alligators good parents?

Alligator dads do nothing for their babies, but an alligator mum is a caring parent. She guards her eggs and helps the young to hatch. The mum may then gently lift the tiny babies in her mouth and carry them to water.

keep warm

The Australian mallee fowl lays its eggs in a mound of earth and leaves. The bird checks the temperature with its beak to make sure its eggs stay warm.

Baby alligator

Quiz time

Do you remember what you have read about baby animals? Here are some questions to test your memory. The pictures will help you. If you get stuck, read the pages again.

3. Are baby snakes dangerous?

page 11

4. When can foals walk?

page 13

1. Why do fawns have spots?

page 6

5. Why do scorpions carry their young?

page 15

2. Are turtles born in the sea?

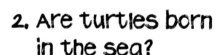

page 9

6. Do sharks lay eggs?

page 17

page 18

7. Do sloths give birth upside down?

page 25 **11. Which bird has the safest nest?**

12. Why are harp seal pups white?

page 27

8. How does a chick get out of its egg?

page 21

9. Do badgers keep their nests clean?

page 21

13. Can rhino mums be fierce?

page 28

10. Do snakes lay eggs?

page 23

Answers

1. To help them blend in with their forest homes
2. No, they are born on land
3. The types that have poison are, yes
4. A few hours after birth
5. To protect them from harm
6. Yes, some do
7. Yes
8. Using their egg tooth to make a hole in the shell, then struggle out
9. Yes
10. Most do, yes
11. The hornbill!
12. To make them hard to spot in the snow
13. Yes they can – they charge at predators

index

A

alligators 29
Arctic 14, 27
Australian mallee fowl 29

B

badgers 21
bald eagles 11
bamboo 27
beaks 19, 25, 29
birds 6, 11, 19, 21, 23, 25
blue whales 4, 15
butterflies 15

C

caterpillars 13, 15
cheetahs 26
chicks 8, 19, 21, 25
chimps 13
cubs 14, 22, 24, 26
cuckoos 25

D

dads 14, 29
deer 6
dens 14, 24
dung 27

E

egg teeth 21
eggs 5, 7, 9, 11, 15, 17, 19, 21, 23, 25, 27, 29
elephants 7, 9, 20

F

fawns 6
feet 19
foals 13
food 7, 17, 19, 26, 27
foxes 24
frogs 5
fur 12, 18

G

gills 5
giraffes 17
gorillas 13, 25
grooming 7
guillemots 23

H

harp seals 27
hatching 13, 15, 21, 23, 29
hedgehogs 29
herds 20
honeybees 19
hornbills 25
hunting 10, 13, 22, 25, 26, 27

I, J, K

insects 7, 9
joeys 8
kangaroos 8
kits 12

L

lions 22
loggerhead turtles 9

M

Macaque monkeys 7
mermaid's purses 17
milk 4, 27
monkeys 7
mouth brooder fish 23
mums 13, 14, 15, 16, 18, 20, 21, 22, 24, 26, 27, 28, 29

N

nests 6, 11, 12, 16, 17, 19, 21, 23, 25

O

octopuses 27
orang-utans 4, 13
ostriches 11
otter pups 10

P

pandas 27
penguins 19
play 10, 13, 22
poison-dart frogs 5
polar bears 14, 27
pouches 8
praying mantises 9
pregnancy 9

R

rabbits 12
rattlesnakes 11
rhinos 28

S

sand tiger sharks 7
scorpions 15
seabirds 23
seas 9
setts 21
sharks 7, 17
sloths 18
snakes 11, 23
spiderlings 17
spiders 17
squirrels 16

T

tadpoles 5
trees 7, 16, 18, 25
trunks 7
turtles 9

V, W

venom 11
Virginia opossums 21
walking 13
warrens 12
wasps 27